POSSIBILITIES

**a simple
reflection**

Amy Churchouse

First published in 2020 by Doing Things Differently

To the extent possible under law, Amy Churchouse has waived all copyright and related or neighboring rights to Possibilities. This work is published from: Australia.

Please attribute any reuse of this work to:
Amy Churchouse
www.doingthingsdifferently.com.au

The invitation

This book will take you on an adventure to discover new opportunities for personal empowerment.

Possibilities makes positive change accessible for anyone, in any situation.

It's an adventure designed to open many doors, reveal new paths, and inspire novel thoughts.

Investigate *Possibilities* with a curious and open mind, to see what you might be able to discover or create. Explore what might be possible with new awareness and a different perspective.

This journey is yours to take – will you overcome barriers, be freed from imitations, or become empowered to make a difference?

These words have been written to create opportunities. Where they take you will depend on how you engage with them.

This adventure starts with a simple reflection …

What can I do with what I have to make things better?

Media delivers negative messages to our screens, papers, and technology every day. These negative messages become negative words between people. Against people.

Advertising is infiltrating all areas of our lives. It's reaching our children. It's changing our behaviour. It's making us notice less, and spend more.

Technology is conditioning us to do things that don't work for us, don't work for each other and don't work for the planet.

'The economy' is thieving our time, our wellbeing and access to our creativity.

And it's all so normal we don't even notice that we are immersed, engaging, participating and even encouraging it to continue.

I noticed …
and I noticed others.

Feeling distressed.

Feeling disempowered.

Feeling disconnected.

We are constantly faced with challenges in the media, our workplaces, our families, in the streets, and on the planet.

That hurt.

That make us upset.

Or even angry...

But what can I do …?

I don't have the time.

I'm too young.

I don't know enough.

I haven't got enough experience.

They won't pay attention to me.

I'm too busy.

I don't know where to start.

I'm feeling distressed.

I'm feeling disempowered.

I'm feeling disconnected.

Things change in our bodies, our minds, our relationships and our lives that mean we can't do the things we used to.

And it hurts.

It makes us upset.

Even angry...

But how can I improve things?

I don't know how.

I'm not smart enough.

I'm too old.

I don't have enough money.

They won't listen to me

I don't have the skills.

I can't because …

I'm feeling distressed.

I'm feeling disempowered.

I'm feeling disconnected.

But I want to try to make things better.

I want to contribute.

I want to make a difference.

So I ask myself ...

What can I do with what I have to make things better?

What could I do?

I could donate some money or some clothes.
Some food or some time.

I could volunteer for something I feel passionate about.
Or to help someone in need.
Or find something I want to learn more about.

I could learn some new skills.
Or a new language.
Learn about another culture.
Or another person.

I could teach someone what I know, what I've learned or about where I've been.

I could share stories, a meal, my car, house or tools. Share my ears for listening. My love, hugs and compassion.

I could join a community and support them. Add numbers to the cause, feel that I can contribute and like I belong.

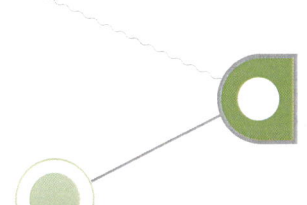

I could start a community and bring people together. Help them feel like they are supported, can contribute and like they belong.

I could do some research. Study and try to find another angle. Grow my knowledge or depth of thought.

I could look after myself. If I'm struggling then I won't be able help anyone else.

I could look after someone else. My sick Aunt. Or her kids. Or their kids.

I could help someone. A neighbour. Or my brother. Or that stranger over there.

I could reach out and connect with others.

'Hi. How's your day going?'

'Hey there. I love your shirt. Where did you find that?'

'Hello. You look like you're a bit lost. Can I help?'

'Hi. I love what you are doing. Can I come and hang out?'

I could look for ways to work together. Cooperate. Collaborate.

Maybe, together, we could find ways to increase our impact.
Or reduce our resource use?
Or both?

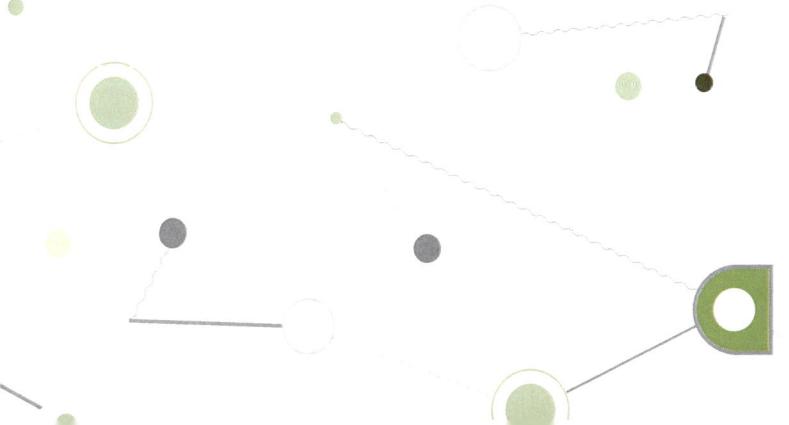

I could think.
About what I am doing.
And why I am doing it.
About whether it aligns with my values.
And about whether I want to keep doing it.

I could dream about possibilities.

A new way of being together?
A new economy?
A new paradigm?
A new understanding between people?

I could discuss those possibilities.

What if ...?
How could we ...?
What would we need ...?
How could we help ...?

All of these things could make things better.

And then I ask myself ...

What can I do with
what I have to make
things better?

What do I have?

I have all of my things.
All of my stuff.
My car, clothes, containers, cushions, crockery, cleaning products, computer,
and candles.
And all of my things that start with other letters too.

I have time.
In between all of the things, and during them too.
There are moments for smiling, chatting, listening, and helping.
Time for thinking.

I have money.
To give away. To enable. To support causes.
To make consumer choices.
To invest in knowledge, wellbeing, growth, and empowerment …

Or someone else.

I have my knowledge, skills and experience to share. To contribute, to build the capacity of others, or shift their perspective.

I have my body for helping, waving, hugging, and dancing.
My mouth for smiling.
My words for complimenting and caring.

I have all of the people I know, my networks and friends.
To learn from, talk to and introduce to each other.

I have my stories to share.
Of joy and pain and problems and people.
Of connection and temptation and touch and terror.

All of these things could make things better.

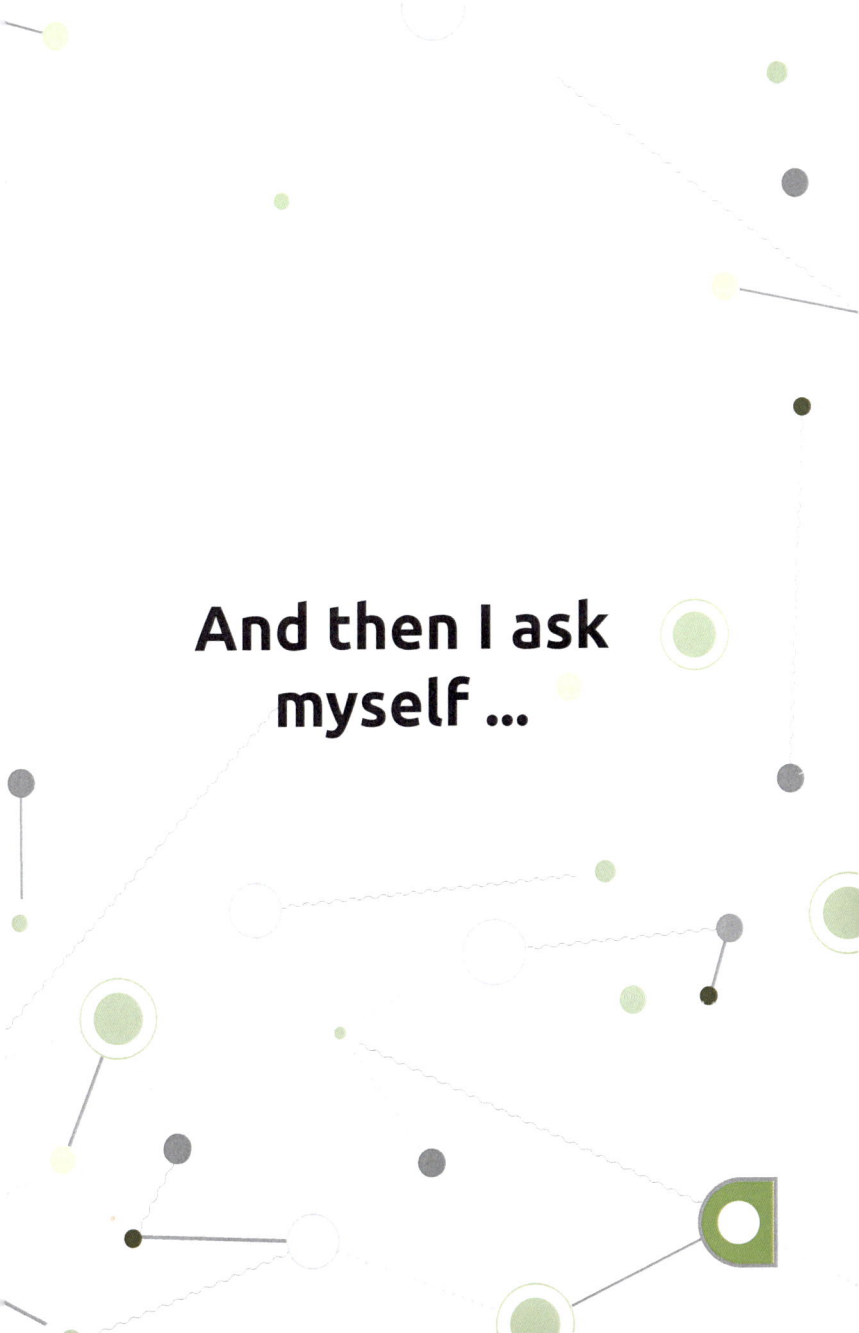

What can I do with what I have to make things better?

What is better?

Healthier.
More efficient.
Less stressed.
Greater self-esteem.
Increased knowledge.

Safer.
More confident.
Asking for help.
Able to overcome challenges.
Increased capacity.

Happier.
More sustainable.
Clearer communication.
Feeling valuable from contributing.
Greater connection.

Easier.
More comfortable.
A reduced workload.
Leaving comfort zones.
Helping more people.

Better.

So now, what are the possibilities?

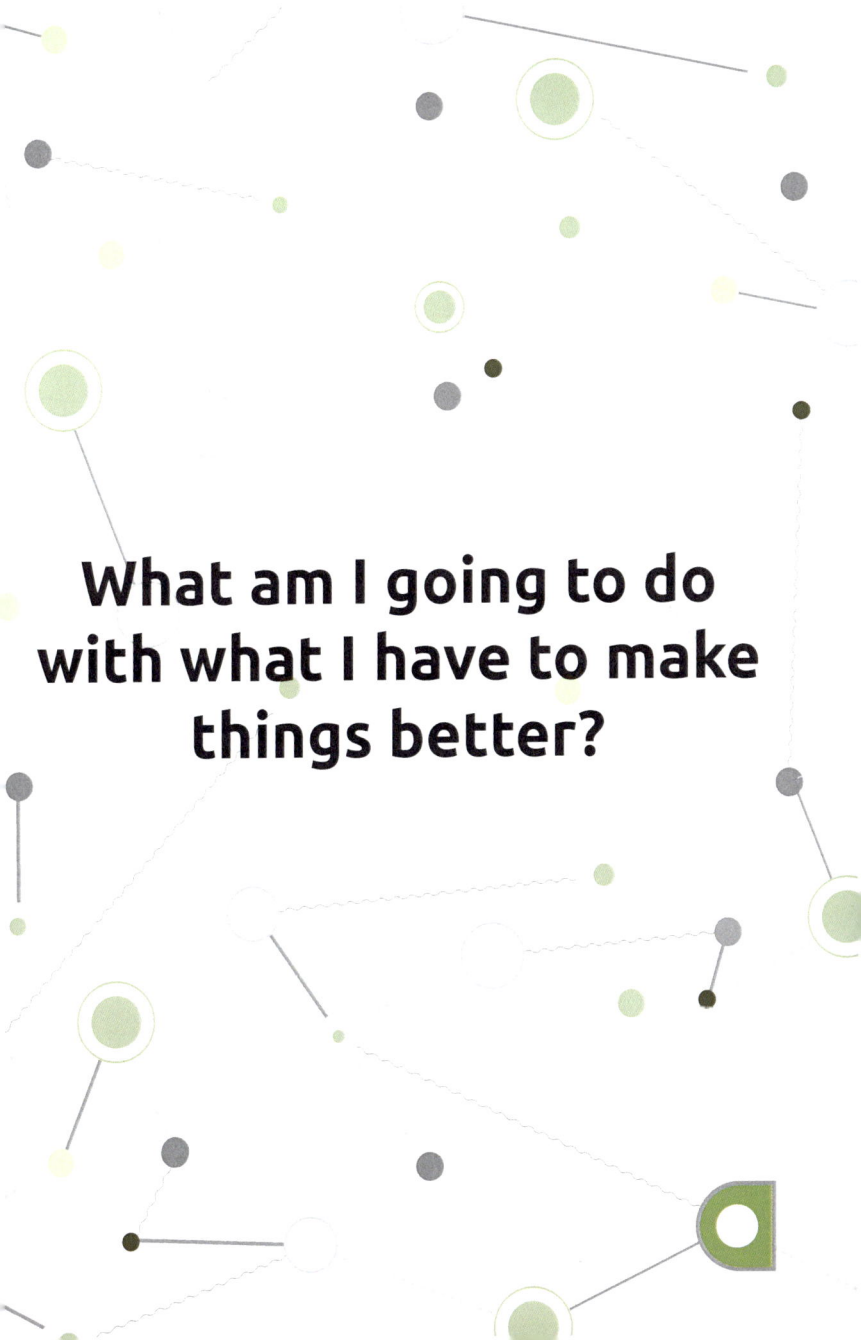

I'm feeling excited.

I'm feeling empowered.

I'm feeling like taking action.

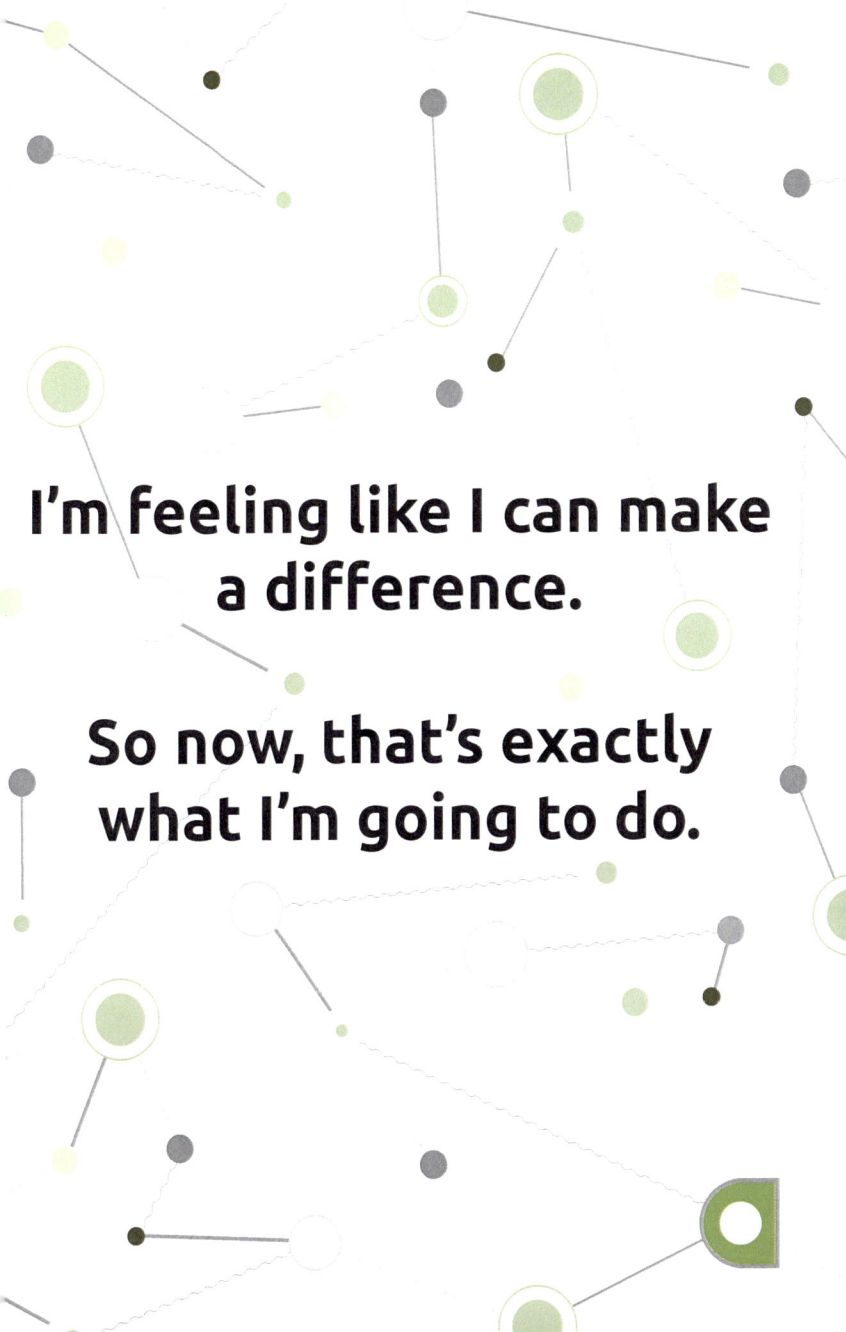

Epilogue

Often after being inspired or having revelations about the possibilities, it is difficult to know what the next steps are or how to get started.

In order to take action, working through the following steps may be helpful to you. As this is your journey, how you decide to proceed is up to you. You may wish to write a list, create a vision board, start a discussion, or connect with others and find people to work with.

You have so much potential for positive impact.

The question right now is, how do you want to use it?

Ask yourself these questions and begin to make a plan.

How do you feel after exploring the possibilities?
What do you want to see happen?
What do you want to change?
Where are you going to start?
What might get in your way?
How are you going to work around these barriers?
Who will be able to help you?
What is the first action you will take?
When will you take it?
How could you evolve your approach to be more effective?

And then do something.
Any one of those things.
That could make things better.

www.ingramcontent.com/pod-product-compliance
Lightning Source LLC
Chambersburg PA
CBRC090837010526
44107CB00052B/1641